W9-CCI-280

The Terrorist Attacks of September 11, 2
J 940

46703

Crewe, Sabrina.

Lake View Public Library

Events That Shaped America

The Terrorist Attacks of
September 11, 2001

Sabrina Crewe and Dale Anderson

Gareth Stevens Publishing

A WORLD ALMANAC EDUCATION GROUP COMPANY

Please visit our web site at: www.garethstevens.com
For a free color catalog describing Gareth Stevens Publishing's list of high-quality
books and multimedia programs, call 1-800-542-2595 (USA) or 1-800-387-3178
(Canada). Gareth Stevens Publishing's fax: (414) 332-3567.

Library of Congress Cataloging-in-Publication Data available upon request from publisher.
Fax (414) 336-0157 for the attention of the Publishing Records Department.

ISBN 0-8368-3399-6

This North American edition first published in 2004 by
Gareth Stevens Publishing
A World Almanac Education Group Company
330 West Olive Street, Suite 100
Milwaukee, WI 53212 USA

This edition © 2004 by Gareth Stevens Publishing.

Produced by Discovery Books
Editor: Sabrina Crewe
Designer and page production: Sabine Beaupré
Photo researcher: Sabrina Crewe
Maps and diagrams: Stefan Chabluk
Gareth Stevens editorial direction: Jim Mezzanotte
Gareth Stevens art direction: Tammy Gruenewald

Photo credits: AP/Wide World Photos: pp. 4, 9, 11, 13, 19, 22, 23, 24, 26;
Corbis: cover, pp. 5, 7, 8, 10, 14, 16 (both), 17, 18, 20, 21, 25, 27.

Printed in the United States of America

1 2 3 4 5 6 7 8 9 08 07 06 05 04

Contents

Introduction

The World Trade Center's two towers rose high above New York City's other skyscrapers before they were destroyed in 2001.

Sudden Attacks

At 8:48 A.M. Eastern Daylight Time on September 11, 2001, a bright clear morning turned into a nightmare. Millions of people in the United States were heading to their workplaces to start an ordinary day. Suddenly, a passenger jet crashed into one of the two World Trade Center towers in New York City. At first, the crash appeared to be an accident, but then another airplane flew straight into the other tower. After that, a third jet hit the Pentagon in Arlington, Virginia. Yet one more plane crashed in a field in western Pennsylvania.

Three Thousand Victims

The crashes were the work of **terrorists**, and they killed about 3,000 innocent people. More than 250 people died on the four **hijacked** planes, 2,797 died in the World Trade Center, and 125 were killed at the Pentagon.

After the attacks, everything changed. Many Americans felt more proud of their country, but others began to question their nation's role in world affairs.

A Missile with Wings

"I looked out my window and I saw this plane, this jet. . . . It was like a **cruise missile** with wings. It went right there and slammed right into the Pentagon. Huge explosion, great ball of fire, smoke started billowing out."

Reporter Mike Walter, who saw the plane crash into the Pentagon

The Targeted Buildings

The Pentagon in Arlington, Virginia, is adjacent to Washington, D.C., the nation's capital.

The terrorists attacked buildings that were **symbols** of American power. The plane that crashed in Pennsylvania was probably meant to hit the White House, where the president lives and works, or the Capitol building, where Congress meets. The Pentagon, as headquarters of the Department of Defense, represents U.S. military strength. It is the largest office building in the world. The World Trade Center's twin towers housed hundreds of businesses and symbolized American wealth. At the time the towers were completed in the early 1970s, they were the tallest buildings in the world—the north tower was 1,368 feet (417 meters) high, and the south tower stood at 1,362 feet (415 m).

Chapter One

Conflict and Terrorism

Different Beliefs

The attacks on September 11 were a terrible shock because they appeared to come out of nowhere. But they didn't. For years, other events had been leading up to the attacks.

All over the world, there are people who see the power of the United States—the world's richest country—as a threat to their countries and beliefs. This is partly because decisions made in the United States often do affect other nations. It is also because people in different countries and of different religions often don't agree about the right way to live. That fact has caused problems for years between the United States and a number of countries in the **Middle East**.

This map shows the countries of the Middle East and neighboring countries, including Afghanistan to the east.

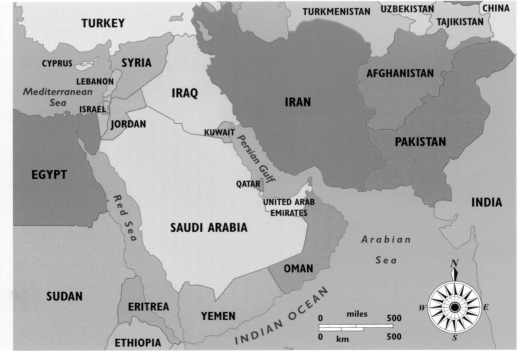

Devout Muslims worship five times a day whether they are at home, at work, or in a mosque such as this one.

The Arab-Israeli Conflict

The Middle East includes several Arab countries, and most Arabs are Muslims, followers of the religion of Islam. Many Muslims in the Middle East resent Americans for a number of reasons. One reason is Israel, a country founded in 1948 in **Palestine** as a homeland for Jews. Ever since its formation, Israel has fought with its Arab neighbors and with the Palestinians who lost control of their homeland. Americans have always helped Israel with money and weapons, and many Muslims dislike the United States for this reason.

Islam

Islam was founded in the 600s by the prophet Muhammad, in what is now Saudi Arabia. Sometimes Muslims have lived peacefully with Jews and Christians, but there are many times in history when the different religious groups have fought.

Today, Islam has about 1.2 billion followers all over the world, and there are more than 5 million Muslims in the United States. Strict Muslims do not like the growing influence of American culture—clothes, food, music, and movies—in the Muslim world. They feel, as many strict Christians do, that modern culture threatens religious values.

The United States and Iraq

Muslims also became angry at the United States because U.S. officials persuaded several nations to stop **trade** with the Middle Eastern country of Iraq in the 1990s. U.S. leaders believed Iraq's **dictator**, Saddam Hussein, was a threat to Americans and that stopping trade would make him give up dangerous weapons. Saddam did not give up any weapons, but thousands of Iraqis suffered and died because they were not getting the food and medicine they needed from other nations. Many Arabs blamed Americans for this suffering.

 ## Saddam Hussein (born 1937)

Saddam Hussein began his rise to power in 1968 and became Iraq's leader in 1979. The next year, he launched a war against neighboring Iran that lasted eight years. In 1990, Saddam invaded Kuwait, hoping to use its oil to make his country stronger. That plan ended with defeat for Iraq when the United States and other nations attacked Iraq in the Gulf War of 1991.

Saddam Hussein at a military parade after the Gulf War.

Until 2003, Saddam kept his grip on power. His secret police and army eliminated anyone who opposed him. The army used deadly **chemical weapons** to kill thousands of Iraqis at a time. Iraq's people starved as Saddam spent the nation's wealth on weapons and palaces. In March 2003, the United States and Britain invaded Iraq to overthrow Saddam Hussein. Within a month, Saddam's long and cruel regime came to an end, but conflict in Iraq continued.

The World Trade Center was first attacked by terrorists on February 26, 1993. This photograph shows the hole made by the explosives used in the attack.

The Rise of Terrorism

In 1979, a few **extremists** began to launch terrorist attacks against the United States. More than fifty Americans were taken as **hostages** in Iran and held in captivity for more than a year. In the 1980s, U.S. embassies, military bases, and travelers abroad were attacked.

The first attack on U.S. soil came in 1993. Muslim extremists packed explosives into a vehicle and parked it in a garage under one of the World Trade Center towers in New York City. The blast from the explosion killed six people and wounded hundreds more.

Al Qaeda

By the late 1990s, many Americans thought that the danger of terrorism had passed. But a secret organization—called al Qaeda—had formed and was growing stronger. Al Qaeda was led by Osama bin Laden, a Muslim extremist who was dedicated to fighting Israel and the United States.

Building a Terrorist Network

Bin Laden was extremely rich and used his money to buy weapons and build a **network** of training camps for terrorists that covered several countries in Africa and the Middle East. The center of al Qaeda's network was in Afghanistan, a very poor and war-torn country on the eastern edge of the Middle East. In Afghanistan, there were plenty of starving Muslims who could be turned into fighters for the cause. The nation also had an extremist Muslim government, the Taliban, that was prepared to offer a home to terrorists.

Osama bin Laden (born 1957)

Osama bin Laden was born in Saudi Arabia into a rich Yemeni family and inherited millions of dollars when his father died in 1967. In his teens, bin Laden came to believe that devout Muslims had to fight a "holy war" against western culture. He gave up the comforts of life as a rich man to join this war, and, as leader of al Qaeda, bin Laden became a powerful terrorist.

Al Qaeda Attacks

In 1998, al Qaeda made its first attack on the United States. In a carefully planned operation, its members bombed U.S. embassies in two cities in Africa, killing more than 220 people.

In response, the U.S. Navy launched powerful cruise missiles against al Qaeda bases in Afghanistan. The attacks damaged the camps but did little to stop al Qaeda, and its network spread throughout the world. In October 2000, al Qaeda bombed a U.S. naval ship in the Middle East, killing seventeen American sailors. By 2001, officials believed the terrorists could be found in more than forty countries. Some of them were working toward the September 11 attacks.

Targeting the Terrorists

"Earlier today, the United States carried out simultaneous strikes against terrorist facilities . . . in Afghanistan. Our forces targeted one of the most active terrorist bases in the world. It contained key elements of bin Laden's network and infrastructure and has served as the training camp for literally thousands of terrorists around the globe."

President Bill Clinton, 1998

This is one of the training camps in Afghanistan where terrorists were trained. The camp was bombed by the United States in 1998 after an al Qaeda attack on two U.S. embassies.

Chapter Two

The Attacks

This map shows the paths and crash sites of the four airplanes that were hijacked on September 11, 2001.

The Plan

The plan for the September 11 attacks called for four teams of hijackers to take control of four passenger jets and fly the airplanes into important American buildings. The impact of the crash would ignite the jet fuel, turning the planes into huge bombs. The planners chose to hijack airplanes flying across the country because these planes had more fuel on board and would make a bigger explosion.

Getting Ready

Hijacker Mohammed Atta was one of the main planners of the attacks. He and the other organizers had to find enough

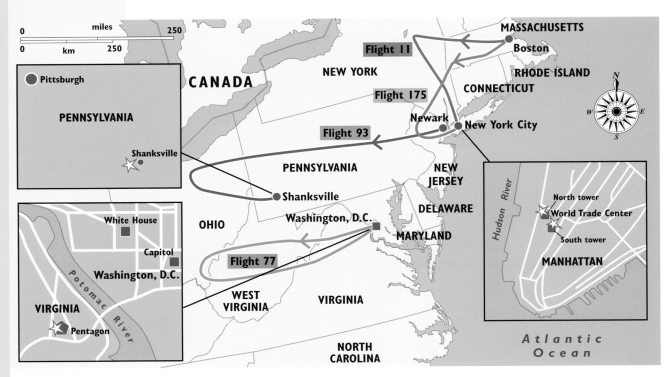

Above the ninety-fifth floor, smoke pours from the World Trade Center's north tower shortly after it was hit. There was no way out for people on the upper floors.

men willing to go to certain death. There were many volunteers ready to die, and nineteen men were chosen to carry out the September 11 attacks.

Some team members needed training to fly jets, and that would take time. Meanwhile, the four teams had to gather in the United States and develop their plan. By late August 2001, the teams were in place.

The attacks were carefully organized. The four hijackings would take place around the same time to prevent officials from doing anything to stop the planes.

The North Tower

The first hijacking on September 11 was of American Airlines Flight 11. At 8.15 A.M., soon after the plane took off from Boston, Mohammed Atta and four companions seized control and headed for New York City. About half an hour later, the jet smashed into the north tower of the World Trade Center between the 95th and 103rd floors. Fires broke out everywhere. All the stairways and elevators to the very top of the building were destroyed, and people above the floors where the plane crashed were trapped.

Like an Earthquake
"The building lurched violently and shook as if it were an earthquake. . . . The building seemed to move 10 to 20 feet in each direction."

Adam Mayblum, who worked in the north tower, remembering the impact

Confusion

People in the building began to escape by taking stairways that were still usable. Some people did not leave, but waited for instructions from emergency workers. Others—on the floors above the crash—had no choice but to wait.

When the first airplane struck the north tower, many people began to leave the south tower as well. A few minutes later, officials declared that the second building was safe and they could return to work. At this point, it was still not clear what was happening. Even people who knew that a plane had crashed into the north tower believed that it was simply a horrible accident.

This series of photographs shows the second attack, as the airplane approaches and then hits the World Trade Center's south tower (on the left in these pictures). A huge hole can be seen in the north tower (on the right), where it had been hit by the first plane.

Flight	American 11	United 175	American 77	United 93
From	Boston	Boston	Washington	Newark
To	Los Angeles	Los Angeles	Los Angeles	San Francisco
Target	World Trade Center north tower	World Trade Center south tower	Pentagon	White House or U.S. Capitol
Passengers/Crew	92	65	64	44
Hijackers	5	5	5	4
Time of Crash	8:48 A.M.	9:03 A.M.	9:37 A.M.	10:10 A.M.

A Second Attack

Fifteen minutes after the first crash, however, the second hijacked jet slammed into the other tower. News cameras, already showing the results of the first crash, were there to record the second one and broadcast it to the shocked world.

Inside the south tower, frightened people crowded onto stairways and any working elevators to escape. Meanwhile, fires raged from the huge hole made by the plane. Debris—pieces of the building, shattered airplane parts, and office equipment—flew to the ground. People, some holding hands, began to jump to their deaths. They chose to fall ninety or more floors rather than face being burned alive.

The Burning Towers

"I could not believe what I was seeing—both buildings were on fire with flames shooting out of them about 100 feet high. Huge plumes of thick black smoke were billowing out of them and when I looked at [the south tower] you could still see the tail end of the jet hanging out of the building."

Eric Levine, who worked in the south tower

A Third Attack

News of the attacks spread across the country. Many horrified Americans were watching the burning towers on their televisions when a third hijacked airplane plowed into the Pentagon in Arlington, Virginia.

The Pentagon, home to thousands of workers, stands five stories high and has five sides. The force of the plane tore a gaping hole in one of the sides, reaching from the ground to the roof. Soon soldiers, office workers, firefighters, and others were doing what they could to find and rescue people. Firefighters also tried to put out the flames from the huge fire that burned late into the night.

Above, President George W. Bush learns of the attacks while visiting a school in Florida.

Right, an aerial photo of the Pentagon shows the damage from the plane crash and the fires it caused. This picture was taken three days after the attack.

Once officials realized that an attack was underway, they tried to stop it. Air Force officers ordered fighter planes into the sky to find the hijacked planes, but there was too little time.

The U.S. government first closed the airports in the New York area and then ordered all airplanes over the United States to land immediately at the nearest airport. For the first time in history, all air

Grounded planes sit at an airport in New Jersey on September 12. Meanwhile, smoke and dust pour from the World Trade Center site.

traffic over the country was stopped. Officials also ordered all people to leave the White House and the U.S. Capitol building in case they were attacked, too.

Danger in the Twin Towers

Meanwhile, hundreds of New York City police, firefighters, and rescue personnel arrived at the World Trade Center. Firefighters streamed up the stairways of the towers to help and comfort people coming down. The rescuers bravely tried to reach and save the people on the upper floors.

The twin towers were quickly becoming more dangerous. The planes had damaged the buildings' strong central cores as well as the steel columns on the outside that supported their massive weights. Fires raging in the towers neared 1,000° F (538° C), a temperature that can bend steel.

The north tower, although the first to be hit, was the second to fall. This series of photographs captured its collapse.

The Towers Collapse

At 9:59 A.M., less than an hour after it was hit, the south tower began to collapse. It only took about fifteen seconds for the entire building to come down. People outside the south tower were blinded by the thick smoke and had difficulty breathing in the dusty air. Falling debris from the tower destroyed another building to the east.

At the north tower, people continued to stream out. Rescue workers realized that even they had to leave. Then, at 10:28, the north tower also came tumbling down.

A Giant Roar

"There was a distant, yet giant crumbling sound. That sound became a giant roar. . . . We saw the upper floors of [the south tower] give way, and break away from the rest of the tower. Then, almost in slow motion, the building fell straight down."

Brendan MacWade, who watched the collapse after escaping from the north tower

"Let's Roll"

At around the same time, another drama was playing out on the fourth hijacked airplane, United Airlines Flight 93. While the hijackers turned the plane and headed for Washington, D.C., passengers learned on their cell phones of the attacks on the World Trade Center and the Pentagon.

As the jet sped toward the nation's capital, the passengers discussed what to do. Passenger Tom Burnett called his wife and told her that they had decided to try to retake the airplane. "If they're going to drive this plane into the ground then we've got to do something," he said. Todd Beamer, unable to reach his wife, spoke with a woman who worked for the phone company. Then the worker heard Beamer say to the other passengers, "Are you guys ready? Let's roll."

Soon after, the airplane's cockpit tape recorder captured sounds of a struggle. There were angry words and screams, and the plane zigzagged. Minutes later, it crashed into an open field near Shanksville, Pennsylvania. All the people on board died in the fiery crash, but the passengers and crew had stopped the terrorists from hitting another building and killing more people.

Passing the Test

"Make no mistake: The United States will hunt down and punish those responsible for these cowardly acts. . . . The resolve of our nation is being tested. . . . We will pass this test."

President George W. Bush, September 11, 2001

This picture of the crash site was taken a year after Flight 93 went down near Shanksville, Pennsylvania.

Chapter Three

After the Attacks

Thousands of people survived the attacks on September 11. Many of them were rescued by firefighters who then lost their own lives as the twin towers came down.

The People Who Died

All 232 passengers and 33 crew members of the four airplanes died in the crashes. At the World Trade Center, 2,797 people died. More than 6,000 were wounded. New Yorkers mourned the loss of 343 firefighters plus several rescue workers and police officers. These brave people had given their lives trying to save others.

At the Pentagon, 125 people were killed and 88 more people were injured. A stroke of "good luck" kept the Pentagon death toll down: the part of the building hit by the plane had recently been renovated. Many workers had not yet moved back into their offices, and so there were fewer people in the area than normal.

The Human Story

At first, for most people, the thousands of victims who died on September 11, 2001, were just numbers. Soon, however, many personal stories emerged. *The New York Times* ran a series of articles honoring those who died by telling the world about them and their lives. Other stories brought home the pain felt by victims' families. Aimee Dechavez spoke for many when she visited the site of the twin towers in 2002. "They never found any part of my brother," she said, "so for us he is still here."

The Survivors

Many of the survivors had scars. Some were physical, but the deeper scars were emotional—the pain felt by firefighters who survived when their friends did not, or by people whose husbands, wives, parents, or children died in the attacks.

On Friday, September 14, churches across the country held memorial services. At these services, people tried to find comfort in their sadness and fear.

Search and Rescue

After the buildings collapsed, workers poured over the site of the World Trade Center. At first, they hoped to rescue people who might miraculously have survived the collapse. After September 12, however, not a single survivor was dug out, and efforts turned to finding victims' remains.

Workers at the World Trade Center continued to comb the site for victims while they began the huge task of cleaning up the debris.

21

Cleaning Up

Another task also began—cleaning up the World Trade Center. It took more than eight months to clear away over 1.6 million tons of debris. The debris came not only from the twin towers, but from nearby buildings that had been destroyed by the towers' collapse.

Rebuilding

The Pentagon did not suffer as much as the New York City site. Only one part of the building had been damaged, and the number of victims was much smaller. Still, many thousands of square feet had to be rebuilt.

Honoring Heroes and Helping Survivors

In Pennsylvania, the people of Shanksville quietly made a memorial to honor the passengers of United Flight 93, who had died when their plane crashed near the town. Across the country, others wanted to do something to help. Many gave clothing, food, and money to help victims' families.

Preventing Another Attack

For the first weeks after the attacks, U.S. fighter planes patrolled the skies above the nation's largest cities. Steps were

The National Guard arrives for duty at a U.S. airport. Every state has a National Guard, a force of part-time soldiers ready for emergencies.

Like all U.S. citizens, Muslim Americans were horrified by the attacks. These two young Muslim Americans attended a peace rally in Dallas, Texas, in October 2001.

taken to tighten security around nuclear power plants and other key danger spots. Security at all airports was tightened as National Guard troops were sent to many airports.

Later, Congress passed a law that put the workers who handled airport security under the control of the **federal** government. The law also required airports to install machines that could x-ray all luggage to look for bombs. The government began hiring more air marshals—armed law enforcement officers—and put them on many flights.

Under Suspicion

After the attacks, police and government agents began to investigate hundreds of Muslims living in the United States. Innocent Americans and visitors to the country were questioned because they were Muslims, of Arab descent, or both. Although most people felt it was important to improve security, some worried that the government might go too far. They complained that holding and suspecting people because of race or religion was unfair and went against American ideas of freedom and justice.

Chapter Four

Around the World

In January 2002, U.S. Navy SEALs explored one of the caves used by terrorists in eastern Afghanistan.

Support from Around the World

The September 11 attacks had shocked people all over the world, and ordinary people everywhere expressed their sympathy. Many pledged their support to fight terrorism. Some cautioned Americans to be aware of how their government's **policies** could hurt others. Everywhere in the world, people feared war and more acts of violence.

War in Afghanistan

On September 20, 2001, President Bush demanded that Afghanistan's Taliban government turn over all al Qaeda terrorists. When the Afghanistan government refused, U.S. and British planes began bombing Afghanistan. Special forces units—highly trained fighters—were sent into the country. After just two months of fighting, the Afghanistan government that had sheltered al Qaeda collapsed.

During the fighting, the U.S. military and its allies in Afghanistan seized vast amounts of weapons and destroyed al Qaeda training camps. They found computer files, papers, and other evidence that told much about al Qaeda.

These prisoners were members of al Qaeda or the Taliban captured by the U.S. military in Afghanistan. They were held at a U.S. military base in Cuba.

Osama bin Laden had disappeared, but over time a few top al Qaeda officials were caught. The head of al Qaeda's military forces was killed in late 2001. Hundreds of terrorist suspects were picked up by local police in many countries around the world.

A Continued Threat

Many terrorists remained at large, however, and attacks continued. Late in 2002, bombs ripped through a nightclub on the island of Bali in Indonesia. More than two hundred people died in the blast, and many more were hurt. More attacks against various targets followed in 2003. It was clear that al Qaeda still remained a threat to the world.

Conclusion

In this Thanksgiving Day parade in 2001, police and other emergency workers carried two huge flags, representing the twin towers, through the streets of New York City.

Rallying the Country

The September 11 attacks united Americans. There was a surge of **patriotism** after the attacks as people rallied to show their love for their country. Americans began flying flags in front of their homes and wearing flag pins on their clothes. More honor was given to people serving in the armed forces. There was renewed respect for police and firefighters, who put their lives on the line for others.

The United States in the World

Some people in the United States and many other countries worried that the September 11 attacks would not change U.S. policies enough. Muslims expressed the hope that the United States would help settle the issue of the Israelis and the Palestinians. In response, President Bush and other U.S. leaders became more involved in peace negotiations between the two groups.

Dividing and Uniting

The division between the Muslim and non-Muslim worlds seemed to grow deeper after the attacks on September 11. At the same time, however, people from all parts of the world began to talk to each other about how to deal with the problems that led to terrorism. They also began working together to end that terrorism, in a worldwide effort that became known as the "war on terror."

Secretary of State Colin Powell (left), President George W. Bush (center), and Secretary of Defense Donald Rumsfeld (right) led the United States in its response to the September 11 attacks.

Time Line

1979	November 4: Americans are taken hostage in Iran.
1990	August 2: Iraq invades Kuwait.
1991	January 16–February 27: Gulf War.
1993	February 26: First attack on World Trade Center kills six people and wounds hundreds.
1998	August 7: Al Qaeda attacks U.S. embassies in Nairobi, Kenya, and Dar-es-Salaam, Tanzania.
	August 20: United States attacks al Qaeda camps in Afghanistan.
2000	October 12: Al Qaeda attack on naval ship U.S.S. *Cole* in Yemen kills seventeen sailors.
2001	September 11: 8:15 A.M.: American Flight 11 is hijacked.
	By 8:45 A.M.: United Flight 175 is in control of hijackers.
	8:48 A.M.: American Flight 11 hits north tower.
	By 9:00 A.M.: American Flight 77 is in control of hijackers.
	9:03 A.M.: United Flight 175 hits south tower.
	By 9:37 A.M.: United Flight 93 is in control of hijackers.
	9:37 A.M.: American Flight 77 hits Pentagon.
	9:59 A.M.: South tower collapses.
	10:10 A.M.: United Flight 93 crashes near Shanksville, Pennsylvania.
	10:28 A.M.: North tower collapses.
	September 14: Memorial services are held for those who died on September 11.
	October 7: U.S. and British forces begin attacking Taliban and al Qaeda sites in Afghanistan.
	December: Taliban government collapses and temporary government is established in Afghanistan.
2002	U.S. government establishes Department of Homeland Security.
2003	U.S. and British troops enter Iraq and overthrow Iraqi government.

Things to Think About and Do

Religious Differences and Similarities

Find out what you can about the beliefs of Jews, Christians, and Muslims. On a sheet of paper, make three columns and list the main points of each religion in one of the three columns. Then compare the three. What is the same? What is different? Are you surprised by your answers? What do you find if you compare any or all of these three religions to Buddhism, for instance, or to Native American spiritual beliefs?

Survivor

Imagine you were working in the Pentagon or in the World Trade Center when the buildings were attacked on September 11, 2001. Describe your experience, how you managed to survive, and your feelings about what happened.

Causes and Conflicts

Terrorists do violent things in order to call attention to their cause and make protests. Do you think any cause is important enough to justify violent actions? What do you think is a better way to deal with conflicts and differences?

Glossary

chemical weapon: weapon that uses harmful chemicals to kill large numbers of people.

cruise missile: computer-guided missile that can fly long distances at high speeds and hit its target precisely.

dictator: leader who has complete power within a country.

extremist: person who has such an extreme view about something that he or she will take dangerous or violent actions.

federal: having to do with the whole nation rather than separate states.

hijack: take control, illegally and by force, of an airplane or other vehicle.

hostage: person captured and held by someone who threatens to harm the person unless his or her demands are met.

Middle East: region of the world from Israel in the west to Iran in the east.

network: large group made up of small units spread over a wide area.

Palestine: region of the Middle East where the nation of Israel was formed in 1948. Palestine was already home to thousands of Arabs when the new country came into being, and this fact causes much of the conflict in the region. In Palestine, there are several ancient sites that are important to Muslims, Jews, and Christians.

patriotism: strong feeling and expression of loyalty to one's own country.

policy: plan or way of doing things that is decided upon and then used in managing situations or making decisions.

symbol: image or object, such as a flag, that stands for an idea.

terrorist: person who performs acts of violence in order to make a political point.

trade: buying and selling of goods, such as food and medicine.

Further Information

Books

Altman, Linda Jacobs. *The Creation of Israel* (World History). Lucent, 1998.

Britton, Tamara L. *The Pentagon* (Symbols, Landmarks, and Monuments). Checkerboard Library, 2002.

Frank, Mitch. *Understanding September 11th: Answering Questions about the Attacks on America.* Viking, 2002.

Gard, Carolyn. *The Attacks on the World Trade Center: February 26, 1993, and September 11, 2001* (Terrorist Attacks). Rosen, 2003.

Wilkinson, Philip. *Islam* (Eyewitness Books). Dorling Kindersley, 2002.

Web Sites

www.911digitalarchive.org A collection of information about the September 11 attacks, including primary sources such as audio and video clips and documents.

news.bbc.co.uk/1/hi/in_depth/world/2001/war_on_terror British Broadcasting Corporation's news site has information on the war against terrorism and background stories on people and events.

www.cnn.com/SPECIALS/2001/trade.center/index.html News network CNN has many stories on the September 11 attacks, al Qaeda, the war in Afghanistan, and similar topics.

www.un.org/Pubs/CyberSchoolBus United Nations' youth web site offers a global perspective on important world issues and information about the UN's work.

Index